CRISIS SURVIVAL RATIONS

CRISIS
SURVIVAL
RATIONS

52 Servings of Hope
To Get You through Your Crisis

J. E. Oppenheim, MA

Publisher: J. E. Oppenheim
Denver, Colorado
United States of America

LIBRARY OF CONGRESS CONTROL NUMBER:
ISBN 1442190183

EAN-13 is 9781442190184

Printed in the United States of America by CreateSpace
Bulk purchases, please contact the author

Dedication

Dedicated to my friend Kevin, whose death led me to write this, and to Julie Anne, Catherine, and Marianne, who have encouraged me with their love. They were there when I first started writing. To Richard, who is waiting for the *in health* part of *in sickness and in health*. He made the book happen. And forever to the Lord, who gave me the strength to keep putting one foot in front of the other. His comfort kept me going.—J.E.O.

You are at the crossroads of your journey.
You may have lost someone
Or something that you loved,
You may have been hurt in a terrible way.
An important part of your life has changed,
And you are on the brink of a new life.

This place can be frightening, painful, challenging.
Remember, though, that in the midst of the dangers,
In the midst of the opportunities,
You are not alone here.
THE GOD OF THE UNIVERSE IS WITH YOU
No matter how alone you feel.
He offers you comfort, encouragement, and hope
In this place, and everywhere you go from here.

Crisis Survival Rations

Ration #	Quick Guide to Topic of Each Ration
1	God's presence - This is temporary
2	God wants the best for me - This is temporary
3	Depression
4	God's compassion
5	The gift of presence
6	Being misunderstood
7	Oppression - Anguish of soul
8	Perspective helps - This is temporary
9	I need to stay in contact with God
10	Anxiety
11	Expectations
12	Scars
13	God's presence
14	God's presence - This is temporary
15	God's presence -Anguish of soul
16	Responsibility for behavior -God is working for my good
17	Depression - Feeling unworthy of love and forgiveness
18	Jesus' suffering -Future hope
19	Keep my eyes on him
20	Choosing to rejoice
21	God's personal care for my needs
22	Brokenheartedness
23	Waiting for God's time
24	Hope in God's promises
25	Not getting out of control
26	Not getting out of control

Ration #	Quick Guide to Topic of Each Ration
27	Anger and mercy
28	God's army fighting for me
29	Turning to God for help
30	This is God's battle
31	The impact of my behavior on others
32	Strength in God's armor
33	Spiritual armor meant for battle
34	Suffering is normal
35	Being faithful to God in hard times
36	God is with me in the furnace
37	No outward marks, but inward growth
38	Things don't always look fair
39	God can use even me
40	God's provision
41	Depression
42	God's care is tailored to my needs
43	Feeling alone
44	Ordinary saints
45	His care isn't always the way I expect
46	Two steps back
47	Seeking out others who are suffering
48	Remembering God's past faithfulness in current crisis
49	God will drive out my opposition at his own pace
50	I can't forgive myself
51	A day holds both good and bad
52	This is the only place I can be right now

"Praise be to the God and Father of our Lord Jesus Christ, the Father of compassion and the God of all comfort, who comforts us in all our troubles, so that we can comfort those in any trouble with the comfort we ourselves have received from God."

2 Corinthians 1:3,4

Ration # 1   God is with me

Now Jacob...went to a certain place and stayed there all night, because the sun had set. And he took one of the stones of that place and put it at his head, and he lay down in that place to sleep. Then he dreamed, and behold a ladder was set up on the earth and its top reached to heaven...And behold the Lord stood above it...Then Jacob awoke from his sleep and said, "Surely the Lord is in this place, and I did not know it." And he was afraid and said, "How awesome is this place!" (Genesis 28:10-13,16,17 New King James Version)

That place was awesome, not because it offered any comfort or beauty, since Jacob had only a rock for a pillow. It was awesome because God was there. God is here with me, in my place of suffering, persecution, and grief. He will allow me to stay here exactly as long as I need to be here. The pain here makes me want to rush away as quickly as my feet will carry me, but **He is here,** in this place. Maybe, if I can remember that, I can stay long enough to grow, or heal, or learn what I need to be His person in that other place where I live in the easier times.

Almighty God, thank you that you never leave me on my own to endure suffering. You are here, even when I do not know it. You are the same God who was with Jacob, and every other believer before or since. You have not changed, and you do not change now. Thank you for your presence. Help me not to miss anything you want to teach me today while I am here.

Ration # 2   God has plans for me and they are good

"For I know the plans I have for you," says the Lord, "They are plans for good and not for evil, to give you a future and a hope." (Jeremiah 29:11 The Living Bible)

In the throes of my pain, I forget that the Lord truly has my welfare on His mind, that He is looking at my future, not just these present, agonizing days. I have to remember that hope is not an emotion. If it were, it would fluctuate with my fragile state. Hope is deeper than that, embedded in my soul. It is at the core of my being, even when I do not feel it, just as my faith is. If I bring it to my daily mind, and let myself see again the reality, it lifts my spirits, even through my tears. It nourishes my starving soul, and gives me a reason to keep on putting one foot in front of the other. I want to engrave this truth on my mind:

I WILL NOT BE IN THIS PLACE FOREVER.
THIS PAIN WILL END.

My precious Lord, thank you that even with all the millions of people on this planet, you still have plans made for me, and me alone. Thank you that the way I feel right now will not last for the rest of my life, because you have a future and a hope for me, your treasured child. Help me to survive until the pain lifts. Help me to remember, when I am drowning in my pain, that there is an end to it. Let it have its way with me, now, so that I will learn what I must to be whole. Show me what I can do today to move forward in my healing.

"He has filled me with bitterness, and given me a cup of deepest sorrows to drink. He has made me eat gravel and broken my teeth; he has rolled me in ashes and dirt. O Lord, all peace and all prosperity have long since gone, for you have taken them away. I have forgotten what enjoyment is. All hope is gone; my strength has turned to water, for the Lord has left me. Oh, remember the bitterness and suffering you have dealt to me! For I can never forget these awful years; always my soul will live in utter shame.
Yet there is one ray of hope: his compassion never ends. *It is only the Lord's mercies that have kept us from complete destruction. Great is his faithfulness; his lovingkindness begins afresh each day." (Lamentations 3:15-23 The Living Bible)*

Jeremiah was as depressed as I have been. As I read the rest of Lamentations, God never once condemns Jeremiah for being honest about how terrible he felt, or for blaming God that he felt that way. God never tried to talk him out of his negative thoughts. God let him feel what he felt, for the time he needed to feel it, so that he could come back to the realization that God was still there for him, and had never left.

God, my Father, you are here with me in my despair. You have not left me, even when I do not feel your presence. You do not hold against me the anger I have felt in this wretchedness. You do not rush me through my depression, here in this place. You created this process for times like these; you know it will end when I am finished with it and ready to let it go. Keep reminding me that this suffering, too, shall pass, just as Jeremiah's did. Thank you that I am not here forever.

3

This I recall to my mind, therefore I have hope. Through the Lord's mercies we are not consumed, because His compassions fail not. They are new every morning; great is Your faithfulness. "The Lord is my portion," says my soul, "therefore I hope in Him!"
(Lamentations 3:21-24 New King James Version)

If your compassion never ends, then you are suffering what I am suffering right now. My emptiness is your emptiness. You feel the powerlessness I feel, the chaos, the overwhelming heaviness. Yet, out of mercy, you have kept what happened to me from being worse than it was and is. That does give me something to be grateful for in this place. You have allowed this to happen to me, but you prevented it from being one iota more destructive than it was; hard as it is for me to believe that right now, you set limits on the destruction, out of your love and mercy for me. I may never understand why this has happened, but I can accept this place more if I remember that you know why, and are in control with plans for my good, through it all.

Thank you, precious Lord, that there is a fresh start to your faithfulness, your loyalty to me, every single day. That it will never be overtaxed or weakened, because it starts again in complete freshness with each new morning, regardless of anything I have done the day before that would exhaust it. Nothing I can do will use it up or take away from it. You have a supply that renews itself from your endless riches every day of my life. And you give it to me now, here, in this place.

Ration # 5   The gift of presence

Now when Job's three friends heard all of this adversity that had come upon him, each one came from his own place...For they had made an appointment to come and mourn with him, and to comfort him. And when they raised their eyes from afar, and did not recognize him, they lifted their voices and wept; and each one tore his robe and sprinkled dust on his head toward heaven. So they sat down with him on the ground seven days and seven nights, and no one spoke a word to him, for they saw that his grief was very great. (Job 2:11-13 NKJV)

What a gift these friends gave to Job in literally coming alongside him, weeping with him, being silently with him in his pain for so much time. Later, of course, they tried to talk him out of his feelings, but for this time, they gave him a week without judgment, of freedom from "helpful" comments or lectures.

How can I communicate to my caring friends that I sometimes would love their presence with me, even if they don't know what to say? Come sit with me, **be** with me, do my errands with me. You don't have to say anything. If I want to talk, I will. If I want **you** to talk, I will ask. What happened to me **is** unspeakable. So don't be afraid of the silence. It is a gift you can give me. The silence speaks more eloquently than any words you can say. Note to self: Is there someone **I** can comfort with my presence, even now?

Lord, you are with me in this desolate place. You are sitting beside me here right at this moment. Help me feel all the truth and power of your presence, and help me be able to ask those who genuinely can, to join us both while we are here, for however long it takes.

We despised him and rejected him—a man of sorrows, acquainted with bitterest grief. We turned our backs on him and looked the other way when he went by. He was despised and we didn't care. Yet it was our grief he bore, our sorrows that weighed him down. And we thought his troubles were a punishment from God, for his own sins! (Isaiah 53:3,4 The Living Bible)

Jesus not only knows personally what rejection, loss and pain are, but he also knows what being misunderstood by others is like. His motives, his actions, his words were constantly scrutinized and misinterpreted. They still are.

How many times he hears his name used as a curse; far more that I have! The worst anyone has ever said about me pales next to the outright venom that has been poured out against him in the past two thousand years. And those who spew the hatred at him are the same people for whom he was voluntarily tortured and killed. By God's standards, my sins are no less heinous than theirs; he suffered as much for **me** as he did for them.

Jesus, my Lord, you have walked in misery and rejection long before me, and are walking these steps with me now. Help me to tolerate being misunderstood and spoken against. Help me to be satisfied with the knowledge that you understand what I am and what is inside me, and it is to you that I must answer, not to my critics. Give me the strength and the endurance to run the race that you have set before me. Today feels like I have broken glass in my shoes, but you know how and when to carry me until the wounds heal. You have walked here yourself.

He was oppressed and he was afflicted, yet he never said a word...yet it was the Lord's good plan to bruise him and fill him with grief. But when his soul has been made an offering for sin, then he shall have a multitude of children, many heirs...and when he sees all that is accomplished by the anguish of his soul, he shall be satisfied...(Isaiah 53:7, 10, 11 The Living Bible)

Lord, will the anguish of **my** soul be satisfied? Will this emptiness, this gaping hole in me be for nothing? My mind knows it will lift, but it feels like an eternal NOW of pain. I wonder about the people I see walking around and looking so normal, so whole. Is that how I look to them? Normal on the outside, with a chasm where my insides should be?

Every now and then, I get a few minutes or an hour when I feel almost normal. When I am really occupied mentally or physically, I can lose myself for awhile, take a vacation from the despair. Then the heaviness comes back, and I wonder if I can carry it another day. My rational mind knows that I will start to have good parts of days, and after more time, whole days of relief, breaking through the cycle of pain I am in now. Knowing that I have gone through other times that seemed unbearable, but came through them, and seeing God's hand in them after the fact, **does** help me to hold on a little longer.

*Jesus, you know what this place is like. You have walked here before me. You walk with me, now, even when I feel absolutely alone. You were flogged, beaten, mocked, and **then** you carried my sorrows and grief. You truly do know what my pain is like, and you do not condemn my weakness or my far-from-perfect ways of coping with the pain. Thank you, a thousand times over, thank you.*

Ration # 8   I need a new perspective

Therefore we do not lose heart. Though outwardly we are wasting away, yet inwardly we are being renewed day by day. For our light and momentary troubles are achieving for us an eternal glory that far outweighs them all. So we fix our eyes not on what is seen, but what is unseen is eternal. (II Corinthians 4:16-18 New King James)

Only when I look at my trials in terms of eternity, do I begin to see them as either light or temporary. I do feel myself being overwhelmed by what my physical eyes are able to see here, in this desolate place. But I must stop limiting myself to the reality of the here and now. The reality that matters, is the one I cannot see with my eyes, but with my heart, my soul, my spirit. That reality has not changed in any way with my current disaster. That reality does not vary with my mood, whether good or bad. That reality is Rock solid.

My precious Lord, fix the eyes of my spirit on the eternity of the Author and Perfecter of my faith. Thank you that you are not shaken by the blasts that have blown so much of me away. Ground me in the truth of your reality, and keep me there through this storm.

Ration # 9   God's personal encouragement to me

May our Lord Jesus Christ himself and God our Father (who has loved us and given us unending encouragement and unfailing hope by his grace) inspire you with courage and confidence in every good thing you say or do. (II Thessalonians 2:16,17 Phillips)

Knowing what God has already given me, and bringing it back to my working mind is one way that God inspires me with courage and confidence in my daily life. I do not dare to go an entire day without some input from his word, and contact with him through prayer. This is true in good times, too, but is especially real to me now, when some days seem so desperate. I do not feel courageous or confident; but I do feel his encouragement and hope. Without his comfort, what other things would I fill those holes inside me with?

Lord, you have already given me your love, your unending encouragement, and unfailing hope by your grace. Thank you for them. Keep me living in the awareness of them. Inspire me with courage and confidence in every good thing I say or do. Help me experience what you have given me, and help me feel the reality of all I have in you, dear Father, when I am feeling empty.

9

Ration # 10   When I'm worried

Anxiety of the heart of man causes depression, but a good word makes it glad. (Proverbs 12:25 New King James)

It is true that at least some of my depression comes from my worries and fears about what **might** happen in this struggle. Being depressed makes me more vulnerable to anxiety, and vice versa. I can choose to withdraw from those who might give me support, or I can put myself among people who I know will give me a good word that will lift me up. The scripture, of course, can give me much help with this, along with other books that can touch my hurting places with comfort.

I must not forget, in my pain, that it does not take much effort to give a kind word to another hurting soul, whose anxiety is weighing him or her down. Whom can I turn to today who will lift me up? Who can **I** reach out to today, who also **needs** lifting up?

*Lord, thank you that you **do** provide respite from the pain in many forms. Open my eyes to see what you are providing for me today. Help me to learn what I need to learn about you and about myself from this time. Help me not to become closed to others who need my encouragement in their pain. Thank you, again, that this time is not forever. My forever is with YOU.*

In Jerusalem there was at this time a man by the name of Simeon. He was an upright man, devoted to the service of God, living in expectation of the Restoration of Israel. His heart was open to the Holy Spirit, and it had been revealed to him that he would not die before he saw the Lord's Christ. (Luke 2:26, 27 Phillips)

The phrase *living in expectation* makes me look at my own expectations. What am I living in expectation of, right now? Is it the same thing I was living for, when my life was easier? Am I expecting to see God be strong on my behalf, or am I living in my fears and my doubts? Am I just barely holding on for the time when I do not feel so powerless or miserable, or when the pain is less?

These are not bad things, but if they are all that I put my hope in, they are limiting what I can let God do through me and to me **now**. And, because of decisions I make or do not make now, habits and attitudes I form now, what I am living in expectation of will affect my future as well. In what ways am I expecting other than what I know God would want for me?

*God, my Father, forgive me for lowering my expectations of you. I realize now how insulting that is to the God of the universe. Thank you for your tolerance of me, and your neverending mercy towards me. I praise you for being so much greater than my expectations, and that regardless of my short-sightedness, you are **never** lowered to my expectations of you. Open my heart to your Spirit, so that I may be led where you would have me go.*

11

Then He [Jesus] said to Thomas, "Reach your finger here, and look at My hands; and reach your hand here, and put it into My side. Do not be unbelieving, but believing."(John 20:27 NKJ)

The ordeal and torture of the crucifixion left visible, ugly scars on Jesus' physical body. As God the Son, he easily could have healed them and removed the marks, but he chose to keep them during the 40 days following his death when he appeared to the disciples and others. He would not have kept these disfiguring marks unless he had a purpose for them.

For one thing, they were a means of identifying that he **was** who he said he was: one who had been put to death in that horrific way, yet who was now alive again. He made no attempt to hide them; rather, He told Thomas to examine them, to touch them, if that was what he needed to do to believe what God had done.

The way Jesus treated them encourages me about the scars I bear physically and emotionally from what I have endured. I do not have to hide them, much as I sometimes wish I could. If they are limiting my life, I can work towards healing the ones that can be healed; but the ones that are permanent are there for a reason, too. They are a part of who I am now.

I am not the untouched person I used to be; I would not want to be that person anymore. My scars identify who **I** am and what I have been through. If God the Son chose to keep and bear his scars to the glory of his Father, who am I not to do the same?

*Lord Jesus, your wounds brought me deliverance and freedom. Your scars are a tribute to what you endured to bring that deliverance. Thank you for what you have brought **me** through **my** wounds. Use them for your glory. Thank you that my pain can honor you, if I let it. Thank you that I am no longer the same person I was when I began this journey.*

*And the Lord said: "I have surely seen the oppression of My
people…and have heard their cry, because of their taskmasters, for
I know their sorrows. So I have come down to deliver them…"
(Exodus 3:7,8 NKJV)*

I do feel oppressed by what happened to me. I feel like I
am at the mercy of my circumstances, my pain, my anxiety, all of
which leave me less able to defend myself from people who want
to overpower me or take advantage of my weakness. Then I am
angry with myself for giving in to them, and angry with them for
exploiting my circumstances. But **God** has seen my oppression,
and has heard my cry. He knows my loss and my pain. He will
come down to deliver me, even when I am too shattered to help
myself. Deliverance is coming, and I am not alone.

*Almighty God, you alone have seen everything that is happening to
me. You will not let my oppression last forever, no matter how
things look right now. You see it, you care about me, you **know
and understand**. This will not last. You will end it. Glorify
yourself in my relief. Deliver me so the world will see your
strength. Not for my sake, but for the honor of your name, Lord.
Open my eyes to the ways you are already being strong on my
behalf. Help me to endure and to honor you in the process.*

When you pass through deep waters, I will be with you; your troubles will not overwhelm you. (Isaiah 43:2 Today's English Version)

I am in deep water. A large hand has held my head under until my lungs were about to burst, then let me up just long enough to gasp one breath before holding me down again. Every ounce of my strength is nothing against that hand. But the Lord sees it all, and will come down to deliver me.

You are bigger and stronger than that hand, no matter how overwhelming it is to me. The forces holding me down will not always have power over me. I am merely **passing through** these deep waters; this is not where I will be spending the rest of my life, despite what it feels like at this moment.

My dear Father, you will not let me drown here. You are not looking elsewhere while I am gasping for air. Help me not to gasp water in place of air when I panic. Give me every breath I need until this is over. Thank you that it will surely end before I give in to the forces around me. Make me feel your power and your strength as I never have before, as you rescue me.

Then they [Joseph's brothers] said to one another, "We are truly guilty concerning our brother, for we saw the anguish of his soul when he pleaded with us, and we would not hear; therefore this distress has come upon us." (Genesis 42:21 NKJV)

Anguish of soul. That phrase expresses it so clearly. The sense of pain beyond mental and emotional, or even physical levels, that comes from the depth of my soul.   Joseph's brothers saw Joseph's anguish, and seemed oblivious to it as they sold him into slavery; later, though, these men remembered it, and knew their part in his pain.

In one moment, Joseph lost his family, his home, his favored status and his freedom. The only thing he did not lose was his God. God was with him in his slavery and in prison, despite how God-forsaken those places surely appeared to him. With all I have lost, I have not lost my God. He is with me, as He was with Joseph.

Dear God, you are still with me, even when my soul is in unutterable pain. I have not lost you. Sustain me here, as you sustained Joseph. Minister to my aching heart. Thank you that you are the same God who brought Joseph out of slavery and prison. Use this time to make me the person you want me to be, as you used Joseph's trials to make him the great leader you wanted **him** *to be.*

15

Joseph said to them, "Do not be afraid, for am I in the place of God? But as for you, you meant evil against me; but God meant it for good, in order to bring it about as it is this day, to save many people alive." (Genesis 50:20 NKJV)

I will never rise to the power that Joseph had, and which these former persecutors feared. But I can choose to see God's hand in turning around my circumstances to good, rather than holding onto bitterness toward those who had no compassion for my suffering when they saw it.

Even though I am powerless to change my past or present reality, I have absolute power over two things: my attitude about the reality, and my behavior in the midst of it. Now, I do not know if Joseph felt brotherly affection while his siblings were selling him into slavery, so many years before this incident. I do not think God expected him to. But there is no reference to his ever having acted with cruelty towards anyone, or excusing unkind behavior because he had been so badly treated in his past. Neither can I ever use my suffering as an excuse to treat anyone else badly, even if they have harmed me. I am absolutely responsible for my actions, regardless of my pain.

*My dear Father, at the very time that Joseph's brothers were meaning evil towards him, you were meaning good from the same heartless act. Thank you that this is true in my life as well. The evil intended by a persecutor is not all that is happening at the moment I am feeling anguish of soul. You are here, working in the midst of it, at **exactly the same time**. I may never see the good you are bringing from it, but you are here, nonetheless, no matter how appalling this place seems right now.*

The righteous cry out, and the Lord hears them; he delivers them out of all their troubles. The Lord is close to the brokenhearted and saves those who are crushed in spirit. A righteous man may have many troubles, but the Lord delivers him from them all; he protects all his bones, not one of them will be broken. (Psalm 34: 17-20 NKJV)

Lord, I need reassurance that my faith in your Son has made me righteous in your sight. My too-frequent giving in to sin, doubts, and weakness make me wonder if these promises must be for someone else. I do know I qualify for the *brokenhearted* part, so I can more easily accept that you are close to me now, in this place. I wonder if it is humility that I have about my abject poverty in the area of perfection before you; or am I so beaten-down by my pain and depression that I feel too flawed to be righteous? Is this what being crushed in spirit is about?

Lord, you know my heart, and do not condemn me for my depression. You know what has brought me here, and my true state before you. You are here, close to me in my brokenheartedness, grieving with me over the pieces of myself I have lost. You know how much loss hurts; you designed grief as the response to it. Help me to feel your closeness in my isolation. Help me today to reach out to someone else who feels the same, and who needs your comfort as much as I do.

17

Therefore we also, since we are surrounded by so great a cloud of witnesses, let us lay aside every weight, and the sin which so easily ensnares us, and let us run with endurance the race that is set before us, looking unto Jesus, the author and finisher of our faith, who for the joy that was set before Him endured the cross, despising the shame, and has sat down at the right hand of the throne of God. (Hebrews 12:1,2 NKJV)

I let myself become so consumed by my suffering that I forget what Jesus voluntarily took on for my sake. He kept his focus on the **end**, the *joy* rather than the ugliness of the shame, the contempt, the physical pain. Can I get myself to do that, even for a little while? What **is** my end? In the final analysis, my future is being with the Lord for eternity. What a celebration that is going to be! Believers from all history, set free from their physical pains and their earthly problems, worshiping their Lord. Worthy is the Lamb, who was slain for me! How can I **not** respond with the most joyous worship I have ever given?

*Thank you, my Lord and my God, for bearing that shame for me. Help me to keep the perspective of what you carried, when I am feeling so alone. You were alone in **your** trials; no one else was with you on the cross. When I think God has forsaken me, I must remember that you had the actual experience of that rejection, while you carried my sin on the cross. When you said, "My God, My God, why have you forsaken me?" it was reality. Thank you that because you endured it, I will never have to, no matter how far away God seems from me right now.*

Therefore…let us throw off everything that hinders and the sin that so easily entangles, and let us run with perseverance the race marked out for us. Let us fix our eyes on Jesus, the author and perfecter of our faith, who for the joy set before him endured the cross, scorning its shame, and sat down at the right hand of the throne of God. Consider him who endured such opposition from sinful men, so that you will not grow weary and lose heart. (Hebrews 12:1-3 New International Version)

The Race

The road is hard, O Lord. The race is long,
And I am so encumbered by sin.
So I lay it aside; now help me on
The race you've chosen for me to run.
And I'll fix my eyes on him, the Author and Perfecter of my faith.
Who called it **joy** to bear the cross for me.
He enables me to run, for he's my hope and he perfects my faith.
And he is treading every step with me.
For he endured the cross; ignored the shame,
Knowing that joy would follow his pain.
Now he's at God's right hand, beside the Throne.
At God's right hand in honor He's won.
So I'll consider him who has endured
So much hostility, Lord, against himself.
And I'll not grow weary, I'll not lose heart.
And I'll run with endurance my race.
And I'll fix my eyes on him, the Author and Perfecter of my faith.
Who called it **joy** to bear the cross for me.
And when the race is run,
I'll rejoice forever more around the Throne.
And join the angels in the victory song.

Author's Note: **This poem is the lyric for a song I wrote a year after my newborn daughter, Elizabeth Joy, died.**

Though the fig tree may not blossom, nor fruit be on the vines; though the labor of the olive may fail, and fields yield no food; though the flock be cut off from the fold, and there be no herd in the stalls—Yet I will rejoice in the Lord, I will joy in the God of my salvation. The Lord God is my strength; and He will make my feet like deer's feet, and He will make me walk on my high hills. (Habakkuk 3:17-19 NKJV)

Despite all kinds of problems, I can choose, like Habakkuk, to rejoice in the Lord, to **joy** in the God of my salvation. If Jesus called it **joy** to die a hideous, humiliating death, surely I can find my joy in the God who sent him to endure it for me. My failures, frustrations, and losses do take on a different perspective when I choose to rejoice. I do not have to provide my own strength to climb the high hills, nor do I need to try to make myself the way I need to be to go where God wants me to go, because God does those things for me. But I **do** have the power to rejoice in my trials, and no one can take that away from me but myself.

Lord God, I rejoice in you as an act of my will, and my heart lifts up to join my will as I do it. Thank you for my salvation. Thank you for the strength you give me. Make my feet, and every other part of me to be the way you want them to be, and take me where you want me to go.

See, I am sending an angel ahead of you to guard you along the way and to bring you to the place I have prepared. (Exodus 23:20 NIV)

God sent an angel to guard the Israelites on their way to the Promised Land (i.e., the place he had prepared). What tenderness and kindness God showed his people! The Lord understood that despite the enormous outpouring of his raw power they had just seen brought upon Egypt to free them from their bondage, they **had** just come out of slavery.

They had been beaten down physically, mentally, and emotionally. At that moment, they were not able to believe or trust as they might have been under different circumstances. God knew that they needed concrete, visible signs of his protection, so that they could have the courage to face the wilderness journey. He knows my wilderness and my journey; will he do any less for me, as I look to him in my day today?

Dear God, you know what my exodus is from, and you know the ways that I need encouragement and visual aids. Thank you for your patience with me in my weakness right now, and your faithfulness to meet my needs, as you met your people's needs long ago.

The Spirit of the Sovereign Lord is on me, because the Lord has anointed me to preach good news to the poor. He has sent me to bind up the brokenhearted, to proclaim freedom for the captives and release from darkness for the prisoners. (Isaiah 61:1 NIV)

Lord you know that I am brokenhearted. You know the extent of my captivity, the darkness, and the imprisonment I have endured. You know what I have come through, and what I have lost. You have come through it with me. You have proclaimed freedom and release. Why do I not always **feel** free or released? Some of my imprisoned parts seem not to have heard the word of my release. God, please bring me release from the ways I am keeping myself a captive.

Lord, you have brought the good news to the suffering and the afflicted. Comfort me in my brokenheartedness. Make me know your presence in ways I have not even imagined before. Thank you that, because of my suffering, I can experience a closeness with you that I cannot know in the easier times. When I feel alone in the prison cell, you are here with me. Use this period of desolation to make me strong, so that I can bring you glory through it. Give me the endurance I need for this time. Bring your release from captivity, and freedom from my imprisonment, in your time. Help me to survive until then.

To console those who mourn in Zion, to give them beauty for ashes, the oil of joy for mourning, the garment of praise for the spirit of heaviness; that they may be called trees of righteousness, the planting of the Lord, that He may be glorified. (Isaiah 61:3 NKJV)

I used to have safety and normalcy. Now, I am grieving, I have ashes, mourning, and heavy spirits. My heart cries out for beauty, joy, and praise to replace them. I want them **right now,** this second, but I must wait for the Giver's time. He knows how long I need to carry this pain, so that it can have its way with me and perform what needs to be done in my life. He has compassion for me in this place, and will bring me periods of relief at those times I feel as if I cannot go on one more moment. The Lord will bring me out at the right time, so that I can be a growing, thriving representative of him, planted by him, to glorify him.

Lord, help me to wait for your time. Help me to last until then. Give me courage and strength to face what I must. Bring glory to yourself from my pain, my grief, my ashes, my despair. Give me relief when I am desperate. Bring me out of this place when I am finished with it.

Ration # 24   Hope in God's promises

Remember your promise to me, your servant; it has given me hope. Even in my suffering I was comforted because your promise gave me life...My sufferings, Lord, are terrible indeed; keep me alive, as you have promised. (Psalm 119:49,50,107 Today's English Version)

When external pressures and pain bury my hope right now, I can rekindle my awareness of that hope by immersing myself in Your promises. Hope truly *does* give me life. What I hope for is what I live for. It keeps me alive, even when I feel like I am being buried alive here. It is an oxygen mask of resuscitation to my suffocation. I will re-visit the promises of God that have comforted me in other times, so that I will have renewed vitality and an oxygen mask in this airless place.

*Spirit of God, fill my collapsed lungs with your respiration. I cry out for your breath in my near-lifeless soul and spirit. Only **you** can fill me, only you can minister to my deadness with your rekindling Self. Only you can heal the parts of me that are dragged down, and crushed, and cut off from air. Take me as limp and battered as I am in this wretched place, and bring me to where you want me to be.*

Set a guard over my mouth, O Lord; keep watch over the door of my lips. Let not my heart be drawn to what is evil, to take part in wicked deeds with men who are evildoers; let me not eat of their delicacies...But my eyes are fixed on you, O Sovereign Lord; in you I take refuge—do not give me over to death. Keep me from the snares they have laid for me, from the traps set by evildoers. (Psalm 141:4,5,8,9 New International Version)

I know that I am much more vulnerable to certain types of temptations right now than I am in easier times. When I am distressed, I am more likely to speak sharply to those I least mean to hurt, or to be intolerant of their weakness. It is too easy to take out my hurt or anger on someone who does not deserve it. That innocent bystander will be just as wounded by me as I am by those who have oppressed me. I become like my oppressors, a thought that appalls me! I must find other ways to vent my frustrations and hurts.

I am responsible for my behavior, regardless of what I am going through. What are some ways that I can decide on **now**, while I am not enraged, to plan how to direct my anger before it builds out of my control? How can I stop myself before I do harm to someone else's spirit? What are on-going ways I can safely drain off my negative feelings so that they do not build up and become out of control? Do I need to go to someone who has hurt me and confront them? Do I need to go to someone I have hurt, and ask their forgiveness?

Lord, I really do need you to set a guard over my mouth and to keep watch over the door of my lips. Make me more aware of the ways I am acting towards the innocent bystanders in my life. Give me your help and strength to stand up to my oppressors, when I need to. Give me the discernment about my behavior, and help me to have your perspective, your direction in all that I do.

Let not my heart be drawn to what is evil, to take part in wicked deeds with men who are evildoers; let me not eat of their delicacies...But my eyes are fixed on you, O Sovereign Lord; in you I take refuge—do not give me over to death. Keep me from the snares they have laid for me, from the traps set by evildoers. (Psalm 141:4,8,9 NIV)

When I am in distress, I am more likely to be tempted to overdo those activities which bring me temporary comfort from the pain. If and when these temporary things become a substitute for the comfort and refuge of God, they are keeping me from getting the **lasting** healing He can bring my heart. Yes, he does provide earthly means to meet my needs, but I cannot let those means become more important to me than they deserve to be. If I let them control or alter my behavior, they are too powerful in my life, and I may need to think about cutting them back, or giving them up completely, if necessary. What am I overdoing these days, to comfort myself?

O Lord, let not my heart be drawn to what is evil. My eyes are fixed on you, O Sovereign Lord: in you I take refuge—do not give me over to death. Keep me from the snares they have laid for me, from the traps set by evildoers.

On my bed I remember you; I think of you through the watches of the night. Because you are my help, I sing in the shadow of the wings. My soul clings to you; your right hand upholds me. They who seek my life will be destroyed; they will go down to the depths of the earth. They will be given over to the sword and become food for jackals. (Psalm 63:6-10 NIV)

David was so angry toward his enemies that he interrupted his loving praise of God to speak about them. He certainly did not mince words about what he wanted to see happen to them. How could he say these words, and think such thoughts, yet still be called a "man after God's own heart"? When I look at his life as it is related in 1st and 2nd Samuel, I notice that he shows remarkably little spite and no cruelty towards any of his enemies.

Probably his most powerful and longstanding enemy was King Saul; yet when David had two different opportunities to kill Saul, he refused to harm him in any way. When Saul's dynasty ended, David sought out every possible relative for whom David could show kindness on behalf of his friend, Saul's son Jonathan.

Could it be that in this Psalm, David was venting his frustrations about his enemies to God, and not intending to take revenge on them? Certainly, he was angry at the betrayals and cruelty done towards him, but he did not seem to act on the harsh words he spoke so often in his poetry. While David was as far from perfect as I am, perhaps one of the reasons he was called a man after God's heart was the mercy he showed to the undeserving people in his life. How often do I show mercy to those who have hurt **me?** How often do I hold a grudge, instead, or speak against them to someone else?

(continued)

27

Lord, I want to be a person after your own heart. Show me the attitudes I must change, and the resentments in my life that are keeping me from being what you want me to be. Forgive me for the grudges that I am holding. Help me to find ways to show mercy to those who have hurt me.

Ration # 28   God's army fighting for me

When the servant of the man of God got up and went out early the next morning, an army with horses and chariots had surrounded the city. "Oh, my lord, what shall we do?" the servant asked. "Don't be afraid," the prophet answered. "Those who are with us are more than those who are with them." And Elisha prayed, "O Lord, open his eyes so that he may see." Then the Lord opened the servant's eyes, and he looked and saw the hills full of horses and chariots of fire all around Elisha.
(II Kings 6:15-17 NIV)

How can my heart **not** be stirred by this display of God's army doing battle for Elisha and his servant? Too often, I see only the outward threat, and not the forces of God ready for battle on my behalf. Like the servant, I need to have my eyes opened to see the reality of these powerful agents of the Lord as they stand at attention to protect me, as they protected Elisha and his servant. **The servant did not have to see them, or be aware of them, for the warriors of God to fight for him.** They were already in the full might and power of the God of the universe. They are here with me, today, just as armed and just as real, whether I see them or not.

*Almighty God, open my eyes to see your forces at work in my warfare. Help me never to forget that more are with me from **your** armies, than are with the opposition. Thank you that you fight on my behalf, even when I do not recognize it, even when I forget to give you credit for the victory.*

29

Word reached Jehoshaphat that "a vast army is marching against you from beyond the Salt Sea, from Syria…" Jehoshaphat was badly shaken by this news and determined to beg for help from the Lord…: "O Lord God of our fathers—the only God in all the heavens, the Ruler of all the kingdoms of the earth—you are so powerful, so mighty. Who can stand against you?…O our God, won't you stop them? We have no way to protect ourselves against this mighty army. We don't know what to do, but we are looking to you." (II Chronicles 20:2,3,6,12 The Living Bible)

I have to admit that I have never had opposition as imposing as Jehoshaphat did in this snapshot from his life. It encourages my heart that he was conscious of his human frailty enough to be badly shaken by the news; it reminds me that I am not cowardly when I am overwhelmed by the news I get.

I need to notice that he turned immediately to God for help. He did not spend days or weeks trying to do battle with his own outnumbered troops. Without hesitation, he turned to the One who was much more powerful than his enemy. What keeps me from doing the same?

O Lord God of my fathers—the only God in all the heavens, the Ruler of all the kingdoms of the earth—You are so powerful, so mighty. Who can stand against you? O my God, won't you stop them? I have no way to protect myself against this mighty army. I don't know what to do, but I am looking to you.

The Spirit of the Lord came upon one of the men standing there—Jahaziel: "The Lord says, 'Don't be afraid! Don't be paralyzed by this mighty army! For the battle is not yours, but God's!' "
(II Chronicles 20:15 The Living Bible)

How can I keep myself from forgetting that what I am going through is not **my** battle, but God's? The facts are:

(1)   This is far more than I can stand up against on my own. I could never begin to succeed in my present state.

--BUT--

(2)   It is not up to **me** to figure out what to do, by my own intellect or resources alone. I do not have to be stronger than my opposition, or to think more brilliantly than my foe. Thank the Lord, I have more to draw upon than my own defeated self.

(3)   Another thing to engrave on my mind: **I have the power and intellect of the Creator of the universe, fighting on my behalf, here and now in this place. I am not alone or unarmed, even when I think I am.**

*O mighty God, how can I ever begin to thank you that, wounded and bleeding and confused as I am right now, it is not my battle, but YOURS. It is fought with **your** resources, not mine. Help me to get out of your way while you do the fighting for me that I cannot do on my own. Great Healer, bind up my wounds and restore my soul in such a way that I can bring glory to you in this fight.*

Ration # 31   Impact of my behavior

While they were stoning him, Stephen prayed, "Lord Jesus, receive my spirit." Then he fell on his knees and cried out, "Lord, do not hold this sin against them." When he had said this, he fell asleep. And Saul [Paul] was there, giving approval to his death.
(Acts 7:59, 60; 8:1 NIV)

[Paul, at the close of his life]: ...At my first defense, no one came to my support, but everyone deserted me. May it not be held against them. (II Timothy 4:16 NIV)

What an impact the stoning of Stephen must have had upon Paul, even though Paul had seemed so uncaring during the act itself. Paul must have thought much about his part in the killing; and Stephen's gracious prayer for his murderers to be forgiven may have reminded Paul of Jesus' words on the cross about his *own* executioners (Luke 23:34). I may never know how others are impacted by my words or actions during times of mistreatment or suffering. Stephen's example inspires me to be mindful of my behavior at this difficult time, even when no one seems to notice.

Lord, let my words and my behavior bring honor to you always, but especially during this time. Do not let me forget that others are listening to my comments, seeing my attitude, observing my actions. Thank you for giving me others' lives for inspiration and encouragement.

In conclusion be strong—not in yourselves but in the Lord, in the power of his boundless strength. Put on God's complete armour so that you can successfully resist all the devil's craftiness. For our fight is not against any physical enemy: it is against organizations and powers that are spiritual. We are up against the unseen power that controls this dark world and spiritual agents from the very headquarters of evil. (Ephesians 6:10-12 Phillips)

       This passage ties together so many truths that other passages have covered: that the battle is the Lord's, not mine; to be fought with his strength, His armor, His resources; that the opposition and the battle are in the unseen realm, not the physical (although the physical world is affected by it). How much of my present suffering is a direct result of this battle? I do not know. But I **do** know that the battle is going on, and that I am commanded as a believer to be ready to pray, preach or die at a moment's notice. I am ready to do any of those, without hesitation. But am I ready to do the day-in/day-out-in-the-trenches warfare consistently, and long-term? I have all the equipment; what is keeping me from being ready? What do I need to let go of or take on to fight this battle?

*Lord, thank you that you have given me all I need to do what you want me to do, and the time you want me to do it. Show me the ways I am letting craftiness of the adversary get through your armor. Help me to feel your boundless strength and protection. Thank you that you are with me in **each day's** battle, that I am not ever fighting on my own.*

Therefore you must wear the whole armour of God that you may be able to resist evil in its day of power, and that even when you have fought to a standstill you may still stand your ground. Take your stand then with truth as your belt, integrity your breastplate, the gospel of peace firmly on your feet, salvation as your helmet and in your hand the sword of the Spirit, the Word of God. Above all be sure you take faith as your shield, for it can quench every burning missile the enemy hurls at you. (Ephesians 6:13-17 Phillips)

As I do spiritual warfare in my daily life, I am encouraged to know how much protection God has given me: five of the six pieces of God's armor are **defensive,** designed to prevent me from harm when I am attacked. God would not have presented armor to me unless he knew that I **would** need it.

Being attacked, then, is to be expected, and should not come as a surprise. So why **am** I surprised when I am attacked? Why do I think that I am being singled out? As a believer, I am in the battle, whether I intended to be or not. God has taken great care to protect my spirit from the forces of evil. The armor is there to be used. My job is to put it on and to resist evil in its day of power. In what ways am I trying to use my own defenses rather than God's armor?

*Dear God, thank you for the armor you have provided me. Help me to see the pieces that I am not using. Thank you that I **am** fully armed, even when I feel like I am alone and defenseless on the battlefield. Thank you that your strength and power are most visible when I am my weakest and most vulnerable. **Thank you that evil may have its day, but you hold eternity in your hands.***

Ration # 34   Suffering is normal

And now, dear friends of mine, I beg you not to be unduly alarmed at the fiery ordeals which come to test your faith, as though this were some abnormal experience. You should be glad, because it means that you are sharing in Christ's sufferings. One day, when he shows himself in full splendour, you will be filled with the most tremendous joy. (I Peter 4:12-14 Phillips)

I do become alarmed at the fiery ordeals I am living through. I have the armor of God for the battle, and God's army to fight for me; why do I forget? Why do I fret as if I were alone against the enemy? Sometimes I **do** remember, and my heart is truly encouraged. As dreadful as the ordeals are some days, however, I have trouble believing that they could be severe enough to connect me with the suffering Jesus endured for the sin of mankind. Looking at his suffering **does** help my perspective of my own problems. It also reminds me how much I am indebted to him for my part in his pain. And I realize that by being connected to him through the commonality of suffering, I can truly feel that he understands my pain, and that I have a better understanding of his.

Lord Jesus, I do take for granted the sacrifice you made for me. Forgive me for this. I know you understand my fears and my worries, and do not judge them. You are the Author and Finisher of my faith, so you will be with me through this all, for as long as it lasts. I am not alone in my fiery ordeals. Thank you for that.

Shadrach, Meshach, and Abednego replied to the king, "O Nebuchadnezzar, we do not need to defend ourselves before you in this matter. If we are thrown into the blazing furnace, the God we serve is able to save us from it, and he will rescue us from your hand, O king. But even if he does not, we want you to know, O king, that we will not serve your gods or worship the image of gold you have set up." (Daniel 3:16-18 NIV)

I have always admired the spirit of these men. They trusted God to rescue them from their execution, but also trusted him even if he did **not** choose to deliver them. They were certainly facing more **heat** in every sense than I ever have. These men had lived through the destruction of their city and their homes, had been dragged to Babylon as teenagers, but had held onto their faith through it all. God certainly had not spared them from suffering, and they surely had their moments of doubt; yet they still absolutely trusted God's plan for them, even if that included fiery death! They stood their ground as believers and refused to back down to idolatrous authority. Can I follow their example today and stretch myself not to compromise under the pressures of **my** world?

Lord, you have given so many examples of believers who were faithful to you in hard times. Help me to grow through the struggles I am having. Help me not to buckle under the weight of my own trials. Thank you that you are patient with me as I fail, and that you will bring me through every trial until I am with you forever.

The king's command was so urgent and the furnace so hot that the flames of the fire killed the soldiers who took up Shadrach, Meshach, and Abednego, and these three men, firmly tied, fell into the blazing furnace. Then King Nebuchadnezzar leaped to his feet in amazement and asked his advisers, "Weren't there three men that we tied up and threw into the fire?" They replied, "Certainly, O King." He said, "Look! I see four men walking around in the fire, unbound and unharmed, and the fourth looks like a son of the gods." (Daniel 3:22-25 NIV)

God did not deliver these men **from** the furnace. He allowed them to be thrown into the heart of it. The heat was intense enough to kill the innocent soldiers who had to throw them inside, so the danger was absolutely real. But what happened? He was brought far more glory by delivering them **within** the furnace! He not only supernaturally intervened so that they could survive the deadly heat, he was **there with them** for this multitude to see; this was a time of a literal appearance of God in human form, perhaps as Jesus, perhaps as the Angel of the Lord. Although my trials are tiny compared with theirs, they are as big to *me* as the fiery furnace when I am in the midst of them. Does my God **not** protect me, and go through them with me, as he did   so long ago?

My dear Lord, you are with me as much as you were with them. Even when my problems feel as menacing or as overwhelming as theirs, you are with me, protecting me. Please help me to be aware of your presence and protection today. My heart needs to feel your balm of encouragement here in the furnace.

So Shadrach, Meshach, and Abednego came out of the fire, and the satraps, prefects, governors and royal advisers crowded around them. They saw that the fire had not harmed their bodies, nor was a hair of their heads singed; their robes were not scorched, and there was no smell of fire on them. (Daniel 3:26b-27 NIV)

The Lord allowed these three to go through the furnace, yet he protected them to such a degree that their physical bodies and clothes did not even **smell** as if they had been in the fire. While their bodies showed no evidence of their time in the furnace, I am sure that their faith was exponentially enlarged by the experience, and that their perspective of suffering was very different after it was over. It is true for me that I have learned from my times of suffering not to be as shaken by many of the smaller stresses that would have left me reeling years ago. Whether or not I have physical, emotional, or spiritual marks from a trial, my capacity to endure has expanded with each new way that I have suffered. I truly am different from where I began, with new resources, new strength, new empathy for others; these blessings may be side-by-side with fresh scars, and bandaged places, but **they are blessings of God**. How can I share this growth with someone around me who is hurting, today?

*Lord, you do have much good to bring out of this place. It helps me to see the ways that I am gaining strength through this experience, even though some days I feel only my weakness. Thank you, Lord, that my weakness is not **your** weakness. Help me to remember that my brokenness allows your strength to be more visible to me and to others. Thank you that you are both my strength and my protection, even when I forget*

Ration # 38   It's not fair

For the Kingdom of Heaven is like the owner of an estate who went out early one morning to hire workers for his vineyard. He agreed to pay the normal daily wage and sent them out to work...That evening he told the foreman to call the workers in and pay them, beginning with the last workers first. When those hired at five o'clock were paid, each received a full day's wage. When those hired earlier came to get their pay, they assumed they would receive more. But they, too were paid a day's wage. When they received their pay, they protested, "Those people worked only one hour, and yet you've paid them just as much as you paid us who worked all day in the scorching heat." He answered one of them, "Friend, I haven't been unfair! Didn't you agree to work all day for the usual wage? Take it and go. I wanted to pay this last worker the same as you. Is it against the law for me to do what I want with my money? Should you be angry because I am kind?" (Matthew 20:1,2;8-15 The New Living Bible)

From childhood, most of us are consumed with wanting fairness *on our own terms.* Occasionally, this leaves us wondering if God really **is** fair in his treatment of us. During these hard times, "Why me?" is usually about my perception that the problems in my life are unfair and undeserved. That can cause me to miss the point of the parable above, which I am coming to believe is really about *accepting God's offer,* **which has remained the same throughout history**: the offer of knowing him personally and spending eternity with him. If I have accepted his gift of undeserved mercy and grace to me, and have the treasure of knowing him, what possible difference does it make to me that others have what appear to be easier lives, or less pain?

(continued)

*Father, forgive me for taking your gifts for granted. I realize that I discount what you **have** done for me when I decide that you are not being fair by **my** standards or my timing. Thank you for your patience with me, and your tolerance of my weakness. Help **me** to look for ways to follow your example and to display mercy and grace to those who are in my life.*

Ration # 39   God can use the fearful

Now the camp of Midian lay below him in the valley. During the night the Lord said to Gideon, "Get up, go down against the camp, because I am going to give it into your hands. If you are afraid to attack, go down to the camp with your servant Purah and listen to what they are saying. Afterward, you will be encouraged to attack the camp." So he and Purah his servant went down to the outposts of the camp.   *(Judges 7:8b-11 NIV)*

The Lord understood that Gideon was afraid; he did not criticize Gideon for it, or tell him that his faith was too weak, or that he was deficient in any way because he was afraid. Gideon had already tested God twice before regarding this attack, but the Lord completely understood that he **still** was fearful, and he offered Gideon relief from it!

God knew Gideon's heart, and his frailty, just as he knows mine. He did not expect Gideon to be ***anything other than he was,*** weak as he was; despite that weakness, or because of it, God was able to use him for a stunning and dramatic victory. Does God not have the same tolerance and kindness towards **me** and my own weaknesses? Can he not use me, no matter **what** condition I am in? Can he not use me in some special ways **because** of my battered spirit?

*Dear God, you are so much more accepting of me than other people have been. You are also more kind than I am to myself, especially now. Help me to remember this truth, and help me to rest in it. Forgive me for the times I have been angry with others for their judgmental attitudes towards me; but **also forgive me for the times I have been just as judgmental of them.** Fill me with your Spirit of acceptance. Use my broken and damaged self in those ways that I can only be used when I am in this condition.*

41

Now the manna ceased on the day after they had eaten the produce of the land; and the children of Israel no longer had manna, but they ate the food of the land of Canaan that year.
(Joshua 5:12 NKJV)

God's timing in his provision for his people was so precise! He knew they could not provide their own food until it could be grown in the normal way, which took months of work and waiting for the crops to ripen. God continued to give the Israelites the manna that they had eaten in the wilderness until **they knew** that they could provide for themselves.

This is the generation of Israelites who had seen their parents and grandparents refuse to trust God about moving into the Promised Land of Canaan, and who had been condemned to wander for 40 years in the desert until everyone 20 years and older had died. This surviving generation had never farmed before, and had no experienced elders to teach them how to plant or cultivate land, so God kept providing food, not merely until their crops came in, but until they had actually **eaten** the produce.

That means he provided manna for them on the morning of the day that they would eat their first food from their labors. They probably could have gone without manna for that day, from a strictly nutritional sense, if God were economizing. But he chose not to stop his extravagant provision even **one day** earlier. Will he **not** care for me in my needs with as much attention to detail? He is the same God he always has been; he will give my soul the nourishment it needs in my wilderness. When I come to my new place, he will provide for me as long as I have a need, or as he did with the Israelites, until the day **after.**

(continued)

Almighty God, make yourself real to me today. Open my eyes to see your faithfulness and your care for me. Help me to feel your presence in my daily life. Thank you that you are working on my behalf, even when I do not know it. Help me to rest in that knowledge. Thank you that you will give me every single day's worth of your provision in every way that I need it.

And Ahab told Jezebel all that Elijah had done [i.e., calling down
fire from heaven], also how he had executed all the prophets with
the sword. Then Jezebel sent a messenger to Elijah, saying, "So
let the gods do to me, and more also, if I do not make your life as
the life of one of them by tomorrow about this time." And when he
saw that, he arose and ran for his life, and went to Beersheba ...
and left his servant there. But he himself went a day's journey into
the wilderness, and came and sat down under a broom tree. And
he prayed that he might die, and said, "It is enough! Now, Lord
take my life, for I am no better than my fathers!" Then as he lay
and slept under a broom tree, suddenly an angel touched him, and
said to him, "Arise and eat"...and the angel of the Lord came back
the second time, and touched him, and said, "Arise and eat..."
                                        (I Kings 19:1-5 NKJV)

Here is one of the most powerful and revered men of God
in the Bible; yet **he** became so depressed that he prayed to die! I
am sure that at least a part of his depression was physical
exhaustion, after all the adrenaline he had poured out during the
confrontation with the prophets of Baal. The passage makes it
clear that Elijah also was depleted nutritionally: twice the angel
personally served him food during this rest.

God did not in any way reprimand him for being depressed,
or even for praying to die. Again as in so many other examples,
God took this person where he was, just **as** he was, and offered
exactly what he needed to be replenished and whole. God was not
offended or threatened by his honest feelings, even when he prayed
to die.

God can certainly handle **my** feelings just as well as he
handled Elijah's at their darkest. He will meet the needs causing
the feelings, and give me the hope to go on, if I allow him to.

                                        (continued)

*Oh, Lord, you know what my limits are, better than I ever could. You know my feelings, whether I express them in words or not, and whether I even **know** them or not. You do not turn against me when I give up and lose hope. You hold me in your power, even then when my hope is shaken. You know exactly how depleted I am, and will send the perfect nourishment to me or will lead me to it. Open my eyes to see how you are doing this today. Do not let my moods make me too self-absorbed to see your hand working in the world around me. Thank you that you will **never** abandon me, wherever I am, however weak I am.*

And the angel of the Lord came back the second time, and touched him, and said, "Arise and eat, because the journey is too great for you." So he arose, and ate and drank; and went in the strength of that food forty days and forty nights as far as Horeb, the mountain of God. (I Kings 19:7,8 NKJV)

Once Elijah's physical needs were met, God stepped in with supernatural provisions that carried Elijah through a journey that was too great for him in his own human strength. I wonder why God gave him this one large serving of nourishment, rather than providing daily meals as he traveled. Elijah surely remembered how the Israelites in the wilderness were given a daily ration of manna that could not be hoarded or stored.

For whatever reason, God knew this man's needs at that singular time of his life, and God knew what he wanted him to learn and to experience on that journey. For whatever reason, feeding him daily would not have helped him as much as this one miraculous serving of food.

God treated Elijah as **an *individual child of his,*** not as the stained-glass figure he has become to us. God sees **me** as an individual, too. He knows my journey and my needs. Will he not meet those needs in the way that is best for me? Can I trust him to take care of me, even now?

*Dear God, you alone know my journey and my deepest needs. You know them better than I do. I do know that sometimes when I think you are not meeting my needs, the reality is that you are not meeting them in **my** time or my way. Help me to trust you more to provide the very best for me, in the ways that I need most.*

So he [Elijah] said, "I have been very zealous for the Lord God of hosts; for the children of Israel have forsaken your covenant, torn down your altars, and killed your prophets with the sword. I alone am left; and they seek to take my life." The Lord said to him: "Yet I have reserved seven thousand in Israel, all whose knees have not bowed to Baal..." (I Kings 19:1-4;14,15,18 NKJV)

In his depression, Elijah probably truly believed that he was the only person left who was faithful to God. God let him express that thought twice (v.10 and v.14). Then God gave him the reality: that in fact there were 7,000 faithful believers still in Israel, who had not compromised or given in to the idolatry of Ahab and Jezebel.

I know I have felt the way that Elijah did, and have felt equally as pessimistic and alone. But there are always other believers around me, who are faithful to God, no matter how alone I feel. Elijah, the mighty prophet of God, was so depressed that he was not aware of the others who might have encouraged him; if even **he** overlooked 7,000 people, then I can be kinder to myself for missing a few of the faithful around me.

I can also be more alert to the fact that my perspective may be colored by my mood, and I can ask for God's help in clearing my vision.

Spirit of God, thank you for moving in my heart, even when I am too upset to feel your touch. Open my eyes to the reality of my condition in this place. Help me to direct my eyes to you, and to the Lord's people who are available to be my comrades-in-arms in the battle. Help me to keep moving forward, despite the depression of my heart. Bring me to others whom I can help and uplift as well.

Ration # 44   Ordinary heroes

...It was their faith that won their reputation for the saints of old...There is not time to continue by telling the stories of Gideon, Barak, Samson, and Jeptha; of David, Samuel and the prophets. Through their faith these men conquered kingdoms, ruled in justice and proved the truth of God's promises. (Hebrews 11:2, 32, 33 Phillips)

The faith Hall of Fame includes such ordinary people! As I read about these people in the books of Judges and Samuel, they do not seem much like heroic figures; but they were obviously heroes in **God's** eyes.

All of them were as weak and flawed as I am, but God saw their faith in him as noteworthy enough to be mentioned by name here. Elijah, who was so spectacular in human and spiritual terms, is not specifically named in this list!

I wonder if God wanted to acknowledge some of these more unremarkable people, because their faith was as important as was the faith of the "stars," whose lives have seemed more impressive to us. The ordinary heroes' struggles, their victories, their pain mattered as much to God as the more dynamic characters in the Scripture. Do **my** pain and **my** battles not matter as much to him?

My dear Lord, thank you that you judge my importance differently than the world does. Thank you that my struggles are just as important to you as these believers' were. Thank you that I have as much value to you and your kingdom as any of these, and that you are as intimately involved with my life as you were with theirs.

And he [Jesus] said to them, "Come aside by yourselves to a deserted place and rest a while." For there were many coming and going, and they did not even have time to eat. So they departed to a deserted place in the boat by themselves. But the multitudes saw them departing, and many knew him and ran there on foot from all the cities. They arrived before them and came together with him.   (Mark 6:31-33 NKJV)

Jesus saw the disciples' need for restoration and privacy, just as he sees my needs. He proposed that they come away with him, and they all went off together. They were looking forward to some precious time alone with their Lord, and what happened?

The crowds beat them to the deserted place, so that it was no longer deserted! Jesus then proceeded to enlist the disciples to help him serve the largest feeding of his ministry. Yet, this came at the time when the disciples were exhausted and depleted, and could not find the time even to eat on their own.

Did Jesus stop meeting their needs to serve the masses? Or, is it possible that he chose to feed their **entire beings** as they were allowed to be a part of this miracle? They surely were able to eat at some time during this event, so their needs were met in a totally different way than they were expecting, and on a scale that they could never have imagined! They had concrete, indelible proof that the Lord would **always** provide for them. They **surely** were uplifted in spirit and encouraged in their weary hearts to participate in such key roles on this day.

Do I ever miss what he is doing in my life for my welfare? Am I looking for him to help me in a different way than he does?

(continued)

*O Lord, I know I limit my experience of you by my expectations of how you should be answering my prayers. Open my eyes to see what you are really doing for me. Help me in my unbelief. Thank you for **always** meeting my needs, even when I do not know that you are. You know my deepest needs and longings better than I know them. Help me to see your work in my life. Help me to give you the credit for what you do for me.*

Save me, O God! The water is up to my neck; I am sinking in deep mud, and there is no solid ground; I am out in deep water, and the waves are about to drown me. I am worn out from calling for help, and my throat is aching. I have strained my eyes, looking for your help...Don't let the flood come over me; don't let me drown in the depths or sink into the grave...I will praise God with a song; I will proclaim his greatness by giving him thanks...When the oppressed see this, they will be glad; those who worship God will be encouraged. The Lord listens to those in need and does not forget his people in prison. (Psalm 69:1-3, 15,30,32,33 Today's English Version)

Today feels like I have been drowning again. Things were going better for a few days, and I was beginning to think that I had passed through the worst of the pain. Then came today, and I feel as if I have started all over again. Will this **never** end? Am I in this place forever? At least I know that David felt the same way I do. God did not strike him dead for saying that he felt God had let him down in his time of need. God knows when I am feeling that way, and does not punish me, either, for my feelings.

Thank you, my Father, for not being offended by any of my feelings. You are greater than my feelings, and will not hold them against me, ever. Please bring to my mind the times when you have come to my rescue, because I know that you have helped me so many times in my life. Help me not to drown in my despair, overwhelming as it is to me right now. Thank you for the easier days, and the rest they gave me from the intensity of the pain. Thank you that there will be other days with lighter loads. Help me to survive until the next one.

Don't let the flood come over me; don't let me drown in the depths or sink into the grave…I will praise God with a song; I will proclaim his greatness by giving him thanks…When the oppressed see this, they will be glad; those who worship God will be encouraged. The Lord listens to those in need and does not forget his people in prison.
(Psalm 69:15,30,32,33 Today's English Version)

There are other oppressed people around me who will rejoice with me when I praise God, and will cry with me when my soul is anguished. I do not draw enough on the comfort that these people can give me right now, in the way that only the fellow prisoners can give.

Why do I get so frustrated and offended by the people who cannot begin to fathom what I am going through, and who offer unfeeling advice or "solutions" to my problems? Why do I keep trying to make them understand what they cannot?

I **must** exert myself to reach out to the others who are also suffering; they can give me absolutely real compassion, if I will only let myself open up to them. God can use them to bring cool water to my parched soul, and I can offer them the same. What keeps me from seeking one of my comrades, right now?

Lord, thank you that I am not alone in my oppression. Lead me to those who can give to me and can receive comfort from me. Open my eyes to them. Open their hearts and mine, so that we can help one another in this place. Thank you that you listen to those in need, and do not forget us in our imprisonment. Please give us the gifts of fellowship and comfort through each other, and draw us closer to you in the process.

Ration # 48   Remembering God's past faithfulness

When David and his men came to Ziklag, they found it destroyed by fire and their wives and sons and daughters taken captive. So David and his men wept aloud until they had no strength left to weep...David was greatly distressed because the men were talking of stoning him...But David found strength in the Lord his God.
(I Samuel 30:3,4,6 NIV)

...my spirit grows faint within me; my heart within me is dismayed. I remember the days of long ago; I meditate on all your works and consider what your hands have done.   (Psalm 143:4,5 NIV— a psalm that was written about a another crisis in David's life)

I am impressed by the way that David coped with this disaster in his life: he discovered the magnitude of the problem, he expressed his sadness instantly and unashamedly, and as it worsened before his eyes, he turned to God for strength.

I wonder if part of his maturity in dealing with such a crisis is that he had already been through so many others, and had seen God be strong for him so many times before. At least some part of his reaction was that he had learned to turn to God quickly, and he trusted the Lord to give him what he needed to endure it.

How many times has God been faithful to rescue me when I was in distress? I will spend some time today listing as many of these instances as I can remember.

O Lord, I need your strength today. I need your wisdom and guidance in these hard times. I know you have been strong for me in the past. I know I can trust you to be strong for me now. Help me in my weakness, as you have helped me before.

Ration # 49   God will rescue me in his timing

[Moses to the Israelites]: You may say to yourselves, "These nations are stronger than we are. How can we drive them out?"...Do not be terrified by them, for the Lord your God, who is among you, is a great and awesome God. The Lord your God will drive out those nations before you, little by little. You will not be allowed to eliminate them all at once, or the wild animals will multiply around you. (Deuteronomy 7:17,21,22 NIV)

The Israelites had good reason to wonder how they were going to do battle with the nations of Canaan, who had become established in Israel's land while they had been in Egypt. They clearly were stronger than God's people at that time. The Lord's method for driving them out was to do so in manageable amounts. There would be worse problems than the Canaanites if they were defeated instantly, as desirable as that would have appeared to the soldiers preparing to battle them.

For some of the big opposition in **my** life, God may choose to free me little by little, as he did the Israelites. Maybe there are worse problems than those I am facing right now, problems that would multiply if I were not so consumed with those I currently have. He does have my attention in ways I never give it in the easy times. The intimacy of desperation feels somehow more **real** in its intensity than the casual fellowship I have with the Lord when my life is more settled.

I have learned ways to manage in the high stress life I am living now; to have that change suddenly could leave a void in my time and my way of life, that could be more stressful to manage than a gradual transition back to normalcy. I must never forget that my God is an awesome God, who will bring me out when I am ready, even if that means little by little.

(continued)

*Dear God, you know how dearly I would love to be free of my struggles. If you choose, in your wisdom, to keep them in my life for a longer time, help me to bear that. You really are a great and awesome God, and you will drive out my opposition in **your** time and **your** way. Thank you that there is victory ahead for us!*

Then he showed me Joshua the high priest standing before the angel of the Lord, and Satan standing at his right side to accuse him. The Lord said to Satan, "The Lord rebuke you, Satan! The Lord, who has chosen Jerusalem, rebuke you! Is not this man a burning stick snatched from the fire?" (Zechariah 3:1,2 NIV)

While I do not understand all of the prophetic meaning of Zechariah's vision, I am encouraged to see the Lord **not allowing** Satan to accuse this believer as they stood before him. I allow Satan to accuse me to myself, when I feel shame for things I have done wrong, things that God has forgiven. It certainly is not the **Lord** who shames me for mistakes I made all the bad decisions of my life. I know that when I am overwhelmed by my problems and my depression, I am more vulnerable to this kind of attack.

Why do I let myself focus so much on my failings? **God** is the authority I must answer to; **he** has forgiven me, and has paid for my sins with his own Messiah's blood. As a believer, I know this, but I see that I sometimes act as if I have higher standards than God's regarding my forgiveness!

I now realize that such an act is blasphemous, setting myself above God, and focusing on myself rather than him. He will not tolerate Satan even to open his mouth against this man, Joshua. Would he tolerate Satan accusing me? Would he tolerate **me** accusing me?

Dear Lord God, you know me, you know my sins. You have forgiven me of so much, and have shown me so much love! You understand that I do not always feel as if I deserve to be forgiven. Please bring me the healing I need in this area. Please give me the discernment to see when I am allowing Satan or myself to berate me for things you have already forgiven. Thank you again and again, for the forgiveness you have so freely given to me. I do accept it, even when I do not feel I deserve it.

In the six hundredth year of Noah's life, in the second month, the seventeenth day of the month, on that day all the fountains of the great deep were opened. And the rain was on the earth forty days and forty nights. On the very same day Noah and Noah's sons, Shem, Ham, and Japheth, and Noah's wife and the three wives of his sons with them, entered the ark. (Genesis 7:11-13 NKJV)

On the **very day** that the world was being destroyed by flood, Noah, his family and the animals were being wonderfully saved in the Ark. I have learned that the same day can hold tragedy and joy. How easy it is to give up on the days that start off with problems, low moods, or bad weather. By giving up, I may miss someone or something that would be a huge encouragement to my heart; or I may not see an opportunity to encourage someone else who needs comfort, which would uplift my own spirits in the process.

The day that my daughter Elizabeth Joy was born and died is the same day on which, a few years later, two of my dear friends had their own precious children, who lived and thrived.

Of course, I still feel sadness when that day comes around every year, but that day holds joy for my friends, and I can honestly rejoice with them for the happy parts of that day. *The Lord made days big enough to contain all the events, good and bad, that he wants them to hold.* I can rejoice and be glad in the day he has made, even if I do it with tears running down my face.

*O Lord, help me not to give up when the days are hard. You are in them, no matter what they are like. And you are with me throughout every moment of them, even when I am not looking to you. You were with Noah and his family on that fateful day: **and you are with me every single day of my life, good and bad.***

Then the dove came to him in the evening, and behold a freshly plucked olive leaf was in her mouth; and Noah knew that the waters had abated from the earth. So he waited yet another seven days and sent out the dove, which did not return again to him anymore...And in the second month, on the twenty-seventh day of the month, the earth was dried. Then God spoke to Noah, saying, "Go out of the ark, you and your wife and your sons and your sons' wives with you." (Genesis 8:11,12, 14-16 NKJV)

Noah was in that ship for almost exactly one year, with the same seven people, to say nothing of the boatload of animals. He must have been **very** eager to leave it, but he waited until the Lord made it clear that he could leave safely. They were in confined quarters, with the heavy, unpleasant duties of feeding and cleaning up after the animals.

These people had a year to think about the fact that everyone they had known would be dead, and that their world would never be the same. These thoughts must have given Noah and his family some hard times during their year in the Ark. But I am absolutely certain that they would not have chosen to be **outside** the protection and shelter of that Ark during the Flood.

The Ark would not have been an easy or comfortable place to be in for an entire year, ***but it was the only place in the world that they would be safe from drowning; it was God's place for them at that time.*** The place where I am is not easy, and is not at all pleasant, but it is God's place for me right now. I must not try to leave it ahead of his time.

(continued)

58

This is the only place for me to be right now:
Anywhere else, I would not be at his side. And
when he brings me out, he will be with me <u>there</u>,
in that other place.

Dear God, thank you for providing this place, even though I
*usually do not want to be here. Because **you** want me here, you*
know why I need to be here; there is no place in the world that
would be better for me right now. Help me to wait for you to bring
me out. Help me not to rush out and miss what you have for me
here.

Help me never to forget
what we have been through here,
in this place.

Topic Addressed Index	Ration #
Anger	16, 27
Anger, resentment	27, 38
Anguish of soul	7, 15
Anxiety	10
Bearing scars	12, 37
Being faithful to God in hard times	35
Being misunderstood	6
Brokenheartedness	22
Choosing to rejoice	20, 51
Day can hold both good and bad	51
Depression	4, 17, 41
Depression	4, 17, 41, 46
Expectations	11, 45
Expectations	11, 24, 45, 46, 48
Faithfulness to God in hard times	35
Feeling alone	43
Feeling unworthy of God's forgiveness and love	16, 50
God is working for my good	2, 8, 16, 21, 52

Topic Addressed Index	Ration #
God uses ordinary people, even me	39, 44
God's armor	32, 33
God's army fighting for me	28, 30, 32,33
God's care for me	16, 21, 42
God's compassion	4
God's faithfulness to me	3, 4, 48
God's perspective	8, 19, 30, 38
God's presence	1, 5, 9, 13, 14, 15, 36, 52
God's promises	2, 18, 24, 30
God's provision	40
God's timing	1, 8, 14, 23, 49, 52
Hope	2, 18
I need to stay in contact with God	9, 19
Personal responsibility for my actions	16, 25, 26, 27, 31, 35, 38, 47
Seeking out others who are suffering	10, 47
Spiritual warfare	28, 29, 30, 32, 33, 34, 49
This is temporary	1, 2, 8, 14, 46, 49, 52
This is the only place for me right now	1, 49, 52

About the Author

J.E. Oppenheim, MA has been a Marriage, Family and Child Therapist since 1990. Professional life includes private counseling practice, leading crisis management workshops across the country, and writing freelance articles for a variety of magazines, including *Church Executive Magazine*.

Devotional writing has been published in *The Secret Place (Winter 2006-2007)* and *Fresh Perspectives*, *L'AboiteIndependent.com, and* transcripts for radio devotionals, broadcast at Taylor University.

Other writing for people in crisis includes:
Crisis? What Crisis?
   Useful Life Skills for People Who Don't Want Them

Strength for Your Journey:
   Encouragement for Christians in Crisis

Miracles Grow:
   Hope Builders for a Challenging Life

Welcome to the Fiery Furnace, Now What?

Email: austen46@gmail.com

Made in the USA